HOW TO DRAW
Bible Figures

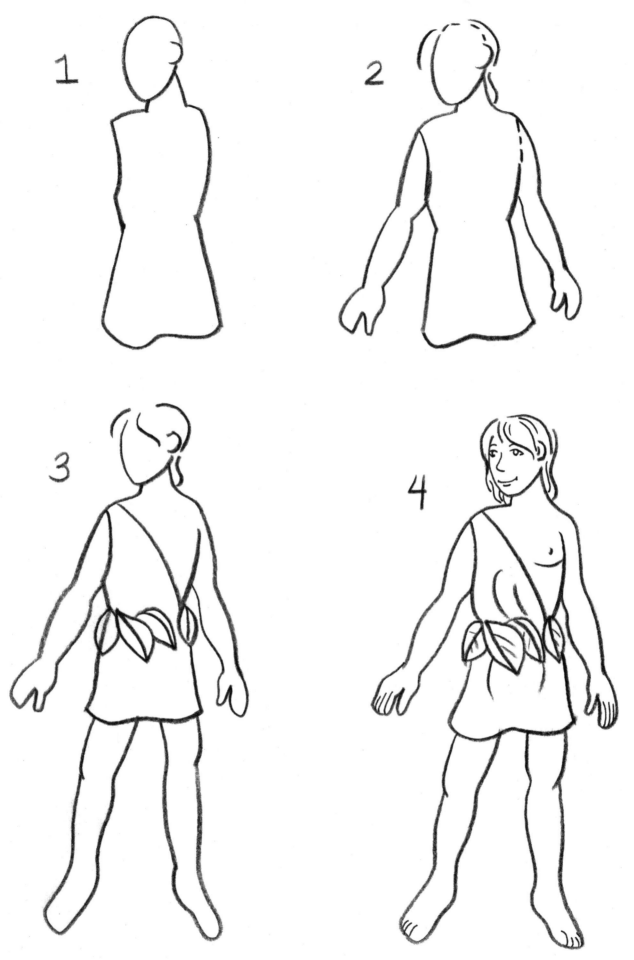

How to Draw
Bible Figures

Barbara Soloff Levy

DOVER PUBLICATIONS, INC.
Mineola, New York

Note

Adam and Eve, David and Goliath, Noah and his ark, and Joseph and his coat of many colors—you'll find these figures from the Bible, and many more, in this easy-to-follow drawing book. To draw each figure, follow four simple steps on each instruction page. Begin with basic shapes such as circles in the first step. For steps two and three, add details to your pictures as shown. The last step shows the finished drawing. It's a good idea to use a pencil with an eraser in case you want to make any changes. There are dotted lines in some of the pictures—just erase these as a final step. You'll find a helpful Practice Page opposite each instruction page, too. When you are pleased with your drawing, you may wish to go over the lines with a felt-tip pen or colored pencil. Finally, feel free to color your drawings any way you wish.

After you have finished the drawings in this book, why not use your new skills to create more drawings of figures and scenes from the Bible? Enjoy!

Bibliographical Note

How to Draw Bible Figures is a new work, first published by Dover Publications, Inc., in 2009.

International Standard Book Number

ISBN-13: 978-0-486-47237-9
ISBN-10: 0-486-47237-X

Manufactured in the United States by Courier Corporation
47237X01
www.doverpublications.com

Practice Page

4   Eve and the Serpent

Practice Page

8   Camels from Noah's Ark

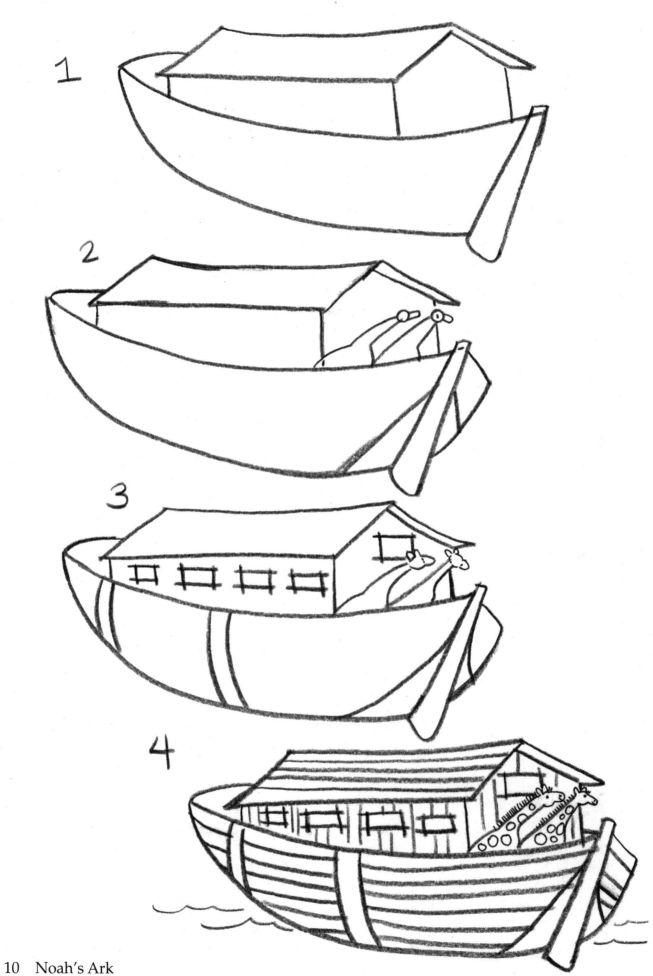

Practice Page

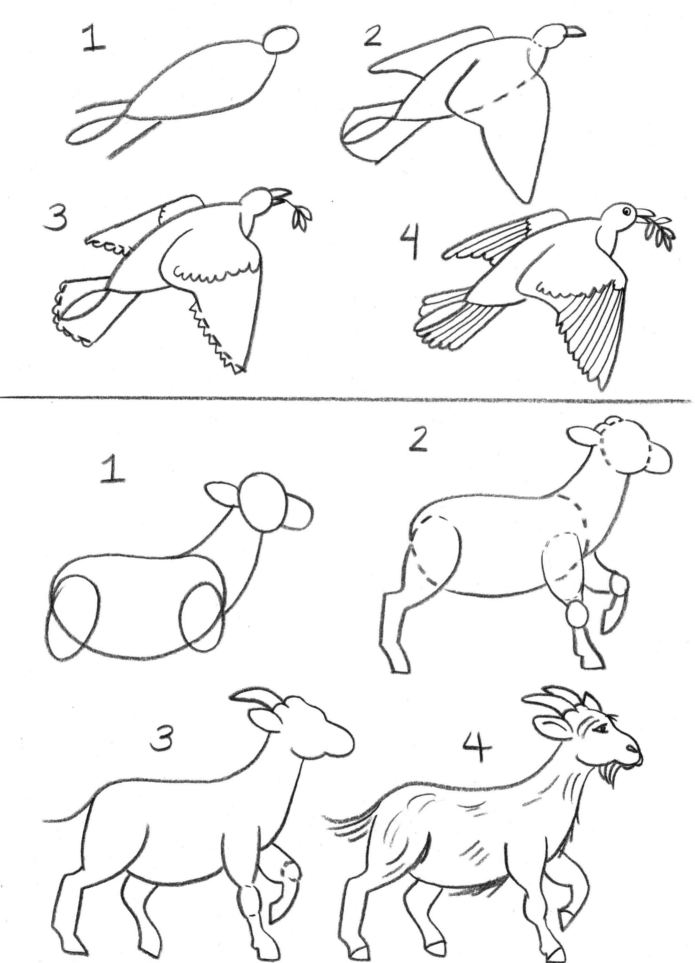

12   Dove and Goat

Practice Page

1

2

3

4

Practice Page

Practice Page

18 Sarah

Practice Page

1

2

3

4

Practice Page

Practice Page

Practice Page

Practice Page

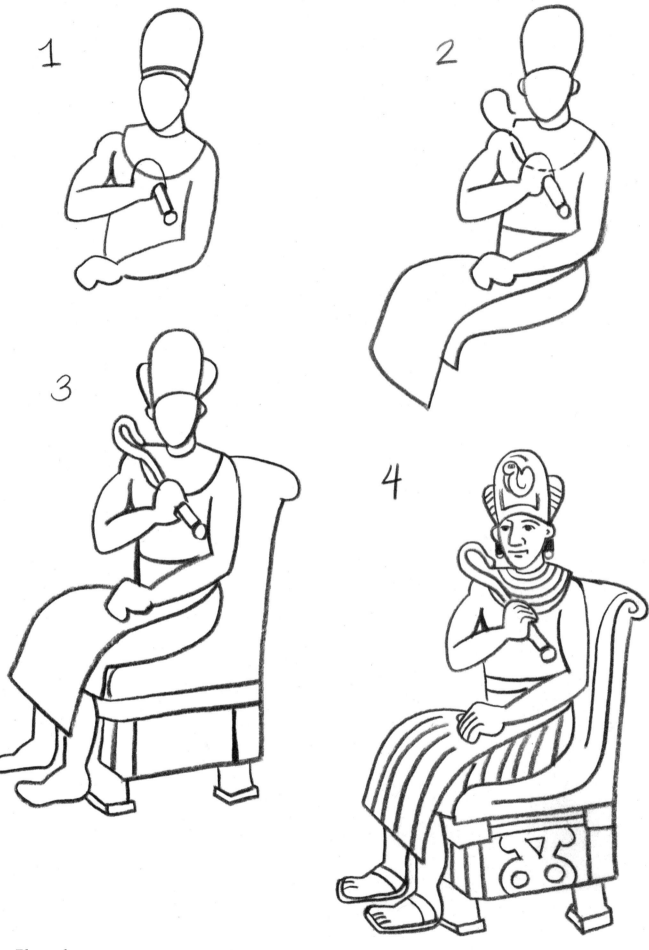

1

2

3

4

Practice Page

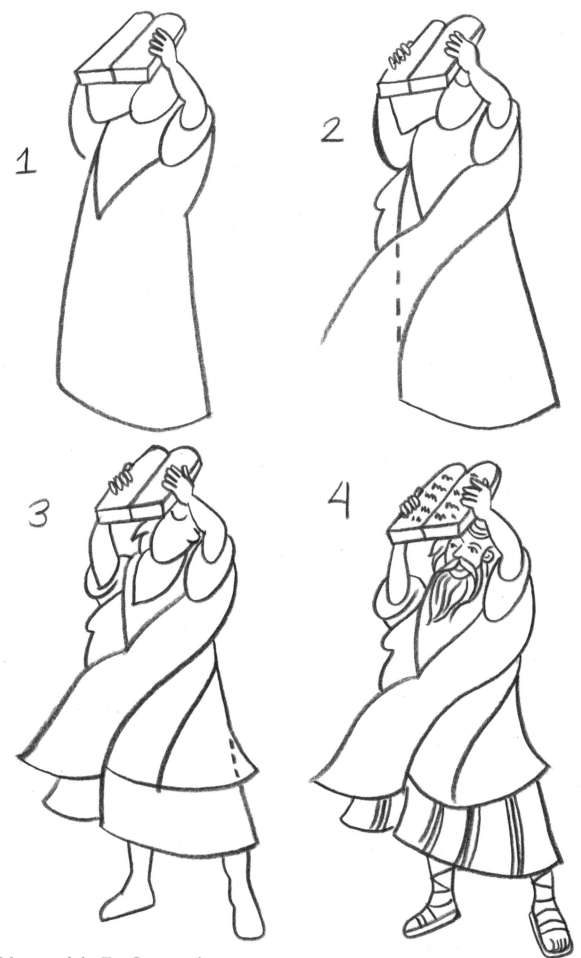

1

2

3

4

Practice Page

Practice Page

1

2

3

4

34 Delilah

Practice Page

1

2

3

4

Practice Page

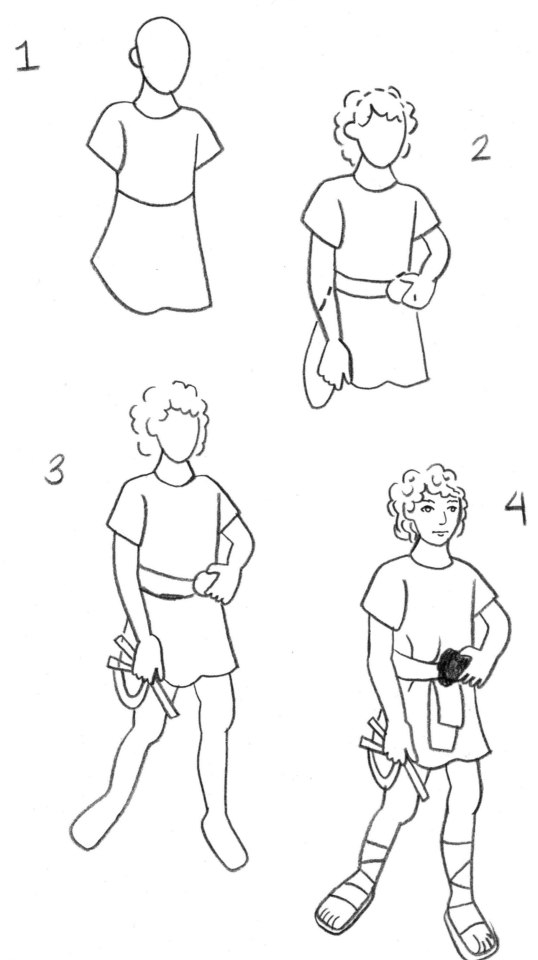

1

2

3

4

Practice Page

1

2

3

4

Practice Page

Practice Page

1

2

3

4

Practice Page

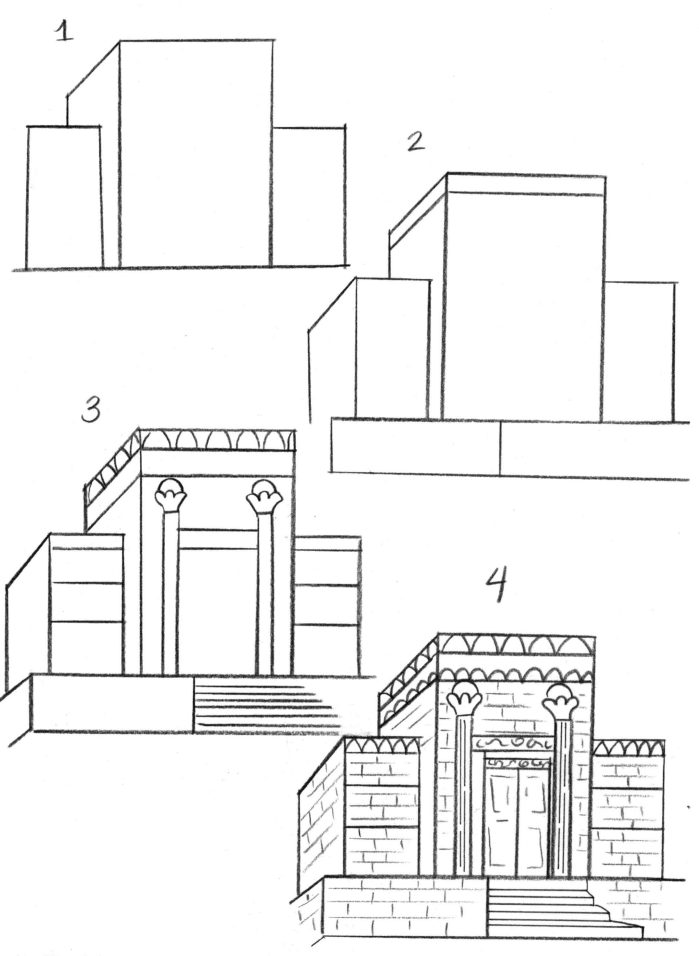

1

2

3

4

Practice Page

Practice Page

1

2

3

4

Practice Page

Practice Page

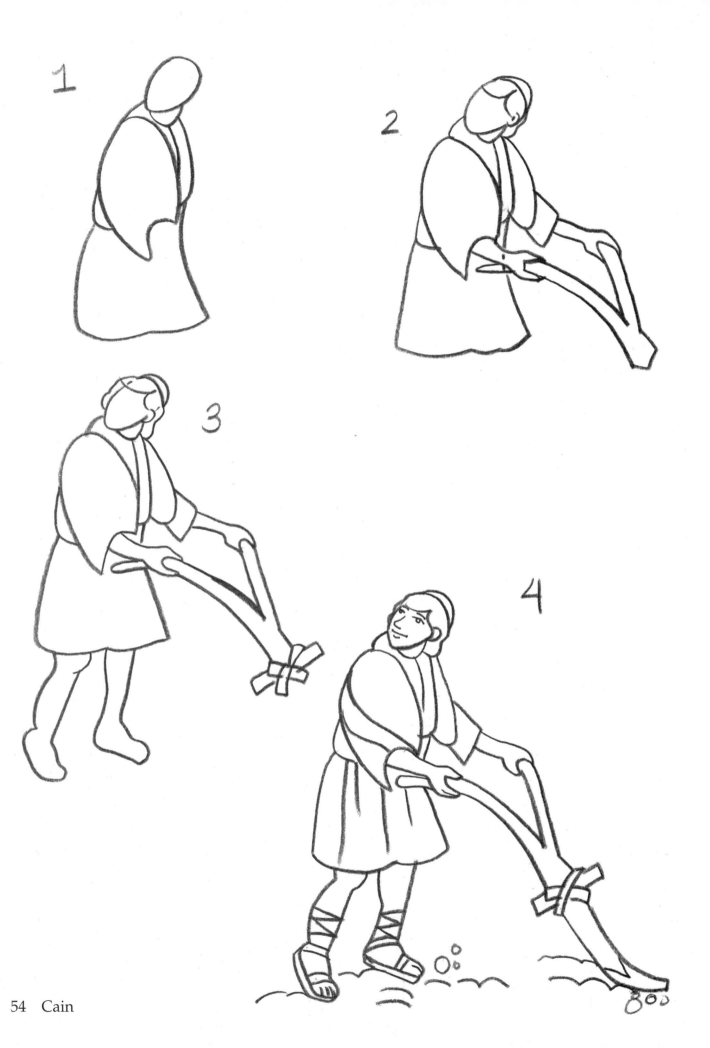

1

2

3

4

Practice Page

1

2

3

4

Practice Page

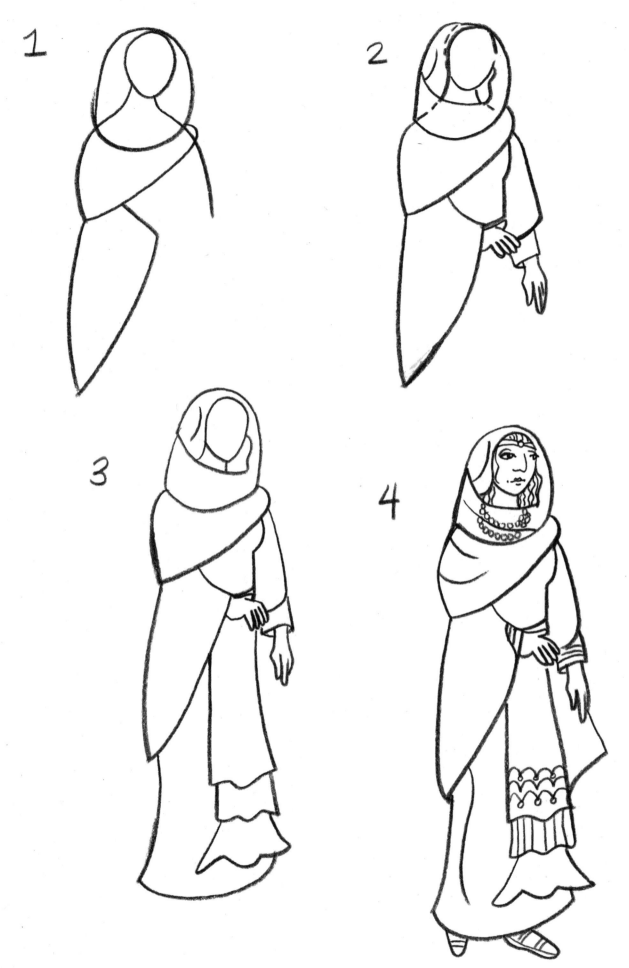

1

2

3

4

Practice Page

1

2

3

4

Practice Page